The Presence of the Lord is in this Place

ISBN-13: 978-1-7343004-0-6

God's Creations Publishing Inc.
P O Box 417
Mexico Mo. 65265
Godscreationpub@yahoo.com

Cover & Layout design by Holly Hyde
Posy Creative
www.posycreative.com

TABLE OF Contents

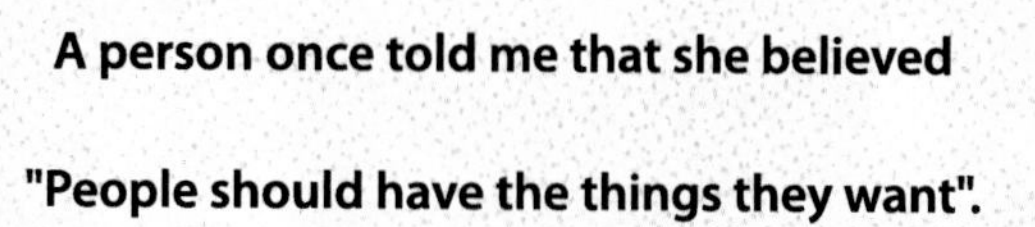

A person once told me that she believed

"People should have the things they want".

Well, not only does she believe it, she works hard to help

them achieve it. *Dana Keller*, I am grateful for your

encouragement, support and lent ear.

PREFACE

This is my first book of many to come and is dedicated to my church family. The reason? So saith the word: 1 Timothy 5:8 – Anyone who does not provide for their relatives, and especially for their own household, has denied the faith and is worse than an unbeliever.

My church family are my relatives in the body of Christ and Faith Walk is the house in which I dwell. "So we, though many, are one body in Christ, and individually members one of another." – Romans 12:5

These are the people who have seen me at my best and who have prayed with and for me when I am enduring the worst. "Bear ye one another's burdens, and so fulfill the law of Christ." – Galatians 6:2

So it is only in obedience to the Word that I do as God has commanded. Luke 12:11-12 says, "When you are brought before synagogues, rulers and authorities, do not worry about how you will defend yourselves or what you will say, for the Holy Spirit will teach you at that time what you should say."

My plan is to allow the Lord to make the plan. My goal is to please and obey the Lord. This I do in the prayer of being like Mary in Luke 10:42: "But few things are needed—or indeed only one. Mary has chosen what is better, and it will not be taken away from her."

For all that partake in the blessings of this book, my prayer is that they spiritually grow, that they learn the personal meaning that the Lord has chosen for their lives and that they walk in it. Not by feeling or sight, but by faith.

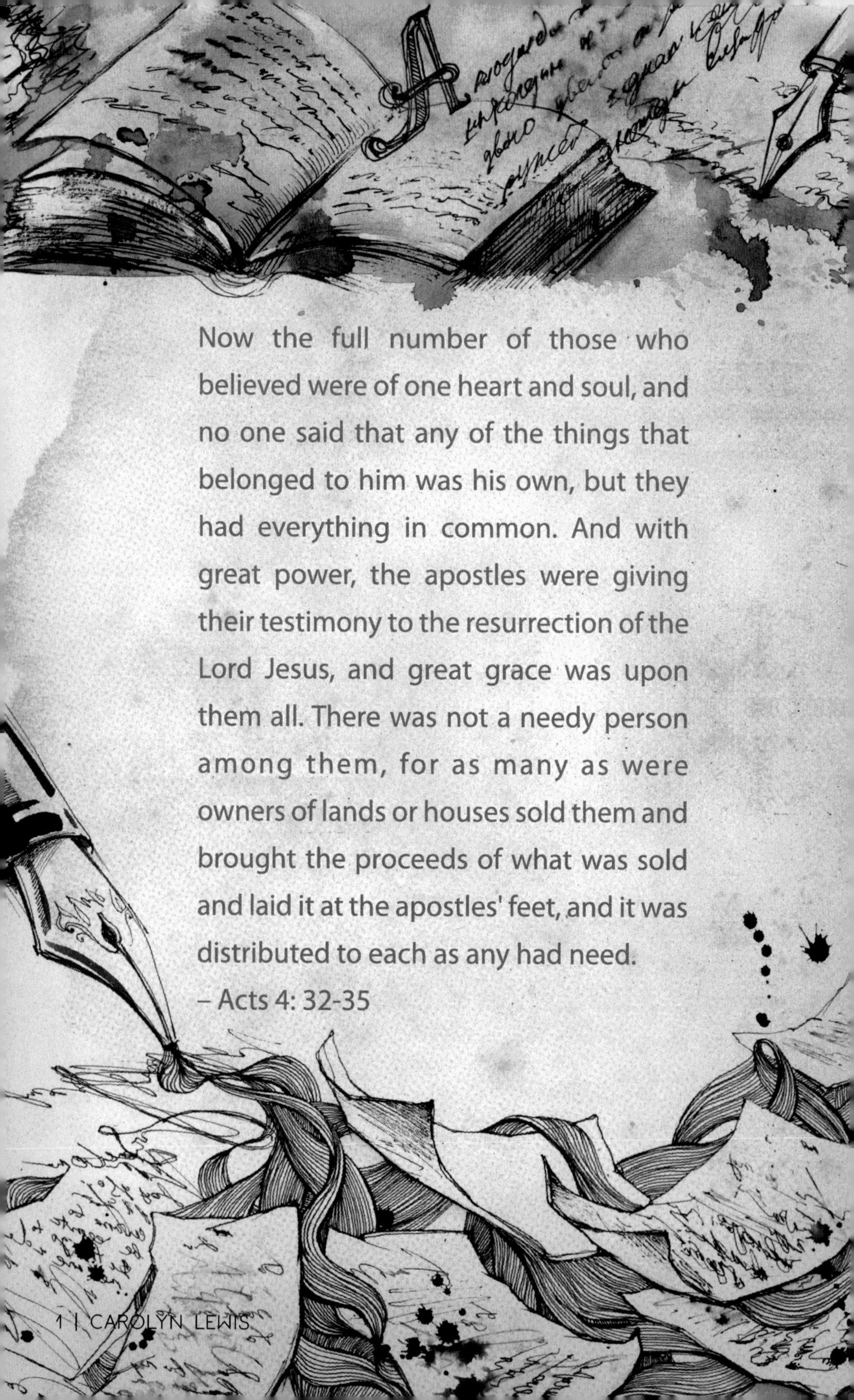

Now the full number of those who believed were of one heart and soul, and no one said that any of the things that belonged to him was his own, but they had everything in common. And with great power, the apostles were giving their testimony to the resurrection of the Lord Jesus, and great grace was upon them all. There was not a needy person among them, for as many as were owners of lands or houses sold them and brought the proceeds of what was sold and laid it at the apostles' feet, and it was distributed to each as any had need.
– Acts 4: 32-35

Dedicated to Apostle Harold G. Long,
Faith Walk Ministries

Many eyes have seen and ears have heard
the anointment in your prophetic words

This is no ordinary talent to speak God's word
Do you not know what it takes to be able to be heard

Not just listen to, yet to also be able to observe...
Observe what God alone has proclaimed as his herd

Spoken with truth that penetrates the most deaf of persons
Not wanting to admit when they must call out and repent

When their inner being is able to be touched with no permission given or reason
to who that they are, yet willing to believe and even allow themselves to be consumed

The being that lies beneath what others see or even what is believed to be
This so-called, "just me"

God's word is truly talking to me? Not through judgments or faults of my wrongs,
Yet through direct knowledge of me. Directly to me through Him?

He that seems to see me, who I never let anyone see
Who are you to be able to speak directly to me – about me

You should not know so much about me to help deliver me
Deliver me to be able to see the real me

How are you able to deliver me from what has incarcerated me
Why are your words truly freeing to me

Why have you been able to show me how to
Receive victory

I am no child. Life is not new to me, yet
A child too views this – what I am now able to see

The words you speak truly have no depths that cannot be reached
How did you come to be able to reach so deep inside of me

Places I dared to explore, and many I came to ignore
Who are you to speak such words to me, to give me the ability
to have such true victory

If knowledge is power, you just taught me, "This is truly my hour!"
"Not an hour", yet a lifetime of power

To truly walk in faith beyond what I could ever believe
I would achieve

The power to defeat any enemy! Just by believing and having faith!
In my God-given testimony!

You taught me who the real enemy was
and it was not me!

I will be called what I was chosen to be
I have purpose and meaning because you showed me!

How to submit and obey
To the only one who could save me

Say yes to God's will is what you instill
Say yes to God's way,
Say yes to God's will

Yes to obey, that is your anthem that must be able to be seen
and not only heard

This Him is you, Apostle Long, that will never be defeated
Apostle Long, much more than a mere man is what God has ordained you to be

You are a true blessing to many,
and that brings the enemy much fear for his destiny

Receive, Repent, Rejoice
That's what you have taught us is true victory

Apostle Long, you are a revealer of truth
and a speaker of God's divine counsel to our appointed destiny

Destiny to unlock doors to places people believe they ought not be
Yet you, Apostle Long, welcome all to partake in God's victory

You judge not the outer
Yet have the vision to see what lies beneath
You teach others how to be healed and
To stay in the perpetration of what God will yet reveal

Apostle Long, you are the him that makes many believe
Just how true God's word is, transforming when you receive

This comes from me and many others which will come back to thee
So don't be in doubt or surprised to know that you are the reason for our victory

To you, we will repay on earth what you will have no need for in heaven.
For to whom much is given much is also due.

God will truly reward you for all you have done.

The Lord answered, "Who then is the faithful and wise manager, whom the master puts in charge of his servants to give them their food allowance at the proper time? – Luke 12:42

NOTES

NOTES

NOTES

NOTES

NOTES

A Phenomenal woman you may believe
But
God-fearing is what you will see
Phenomenal not because I am a woman
But
Because God made me
First Lady
Was what God ordained for me to be
First Lady does not imply
Only lady to me
God chosen and divine
Through grace and mercy
Yes
God did design
Molded me into what you now see
Through God's grace and mercy
Yes
I am a living testimony
First Lady means to me
I am to first be a lady
As a Witness of God
To the ladies
Govern before me
I can not always allow
There to be sway in my hips
Or
Things on my lips
That ought not to be
I am in no way flawless
Or
Without Sin
But
That is between me and God
And
The relationship with God, I have within
I am First Lady yes, ordained by thee
And
First Lady is who I will always be

written for First Lady Deborah Long

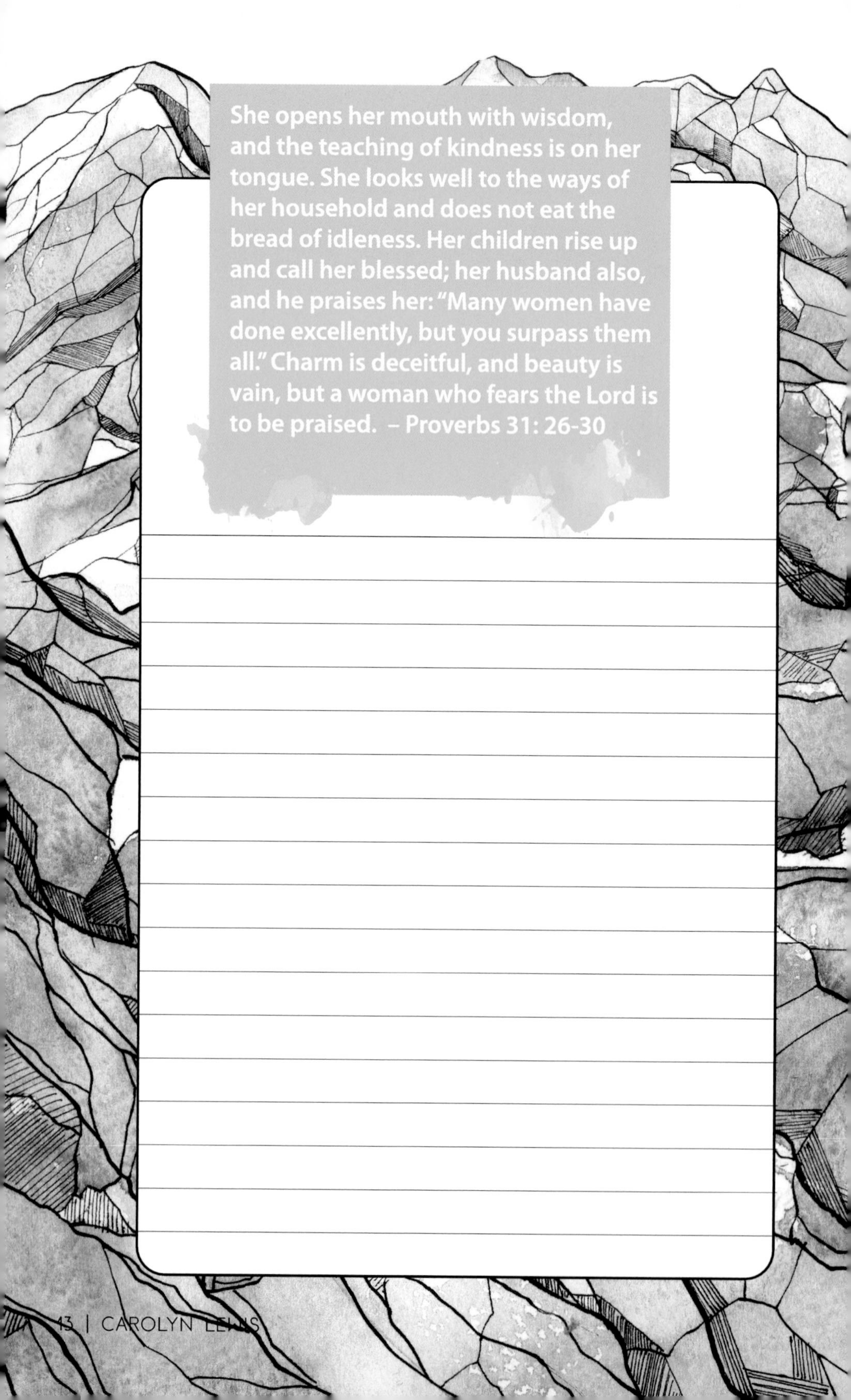
She opens her mouth with wisdom, and the teaching of kindness is on her tongue. She looks well to the ways of her household and does not eat the bread of idleness. Her children rise up and call her blessed; her husband also, and he praises her: "Many women have done excellently, but you surpass them all." Charm is deceitful, and beauty is vain, but a woman who fears the Lord is to be praised. – Proverbs 31: 26-30

NOTES

NOTES

NOTES

NOTES

NOTES

When She Sang

written for Kesha Long

A voice able to be heard by the angels above
Sent down from a heavenly view

So we would be able to hear
What they already knew

A voice that sounds like
If imagined would be Love

A voice that has a spirit that dwells within
The Holy Spirit falls like rain when she's able to sang

Wounded souls feel the glory,
That they once were able to control

Yet, the Glory is beheld
From this earthly soul

Evil spirits go into shame
To even be in the presence
Of what God has ordained

Her voice fights battles the devil believed, he had gained
That is until she calls out his name

Jesus, Jesus,
Who is called by many a name

Souls cry out – a victory
For the release of stains, unseen by human eyes

When if left , will lead many to their demise

Yes, in Jesus name
Yes, Jesus is heard in every word

As she proclaimed the Word
In every word she sang

Glory, Glory is in God's Word as we proclaim
"Lord, she can sang"

Sing to the LORD! Give praise to the LORD! He rescues the life of the needy from the hands of the wicked. Psalms 7:17 I will praise the Lord according to His righteousness and will sing praise to the name of the Lord Most High.
– Jeremiah 20:13

NOTES

NOTES

NOTES

What Is the Need

Is need another word transposed to mean greed

Do I need new clothes
If
I have clothes I have yet to wear

Do I need food when my freezer is not bare

Is my need based on my greed in which I have transposed

What is the need

Is it greed that makes me put 20% in the collection plate

Is it greed that allows me to stay at church late

Is it greed that allows me to pray until I am running late

What is the need

Is it need that tells me I deserve everything I have

Is it need when I am able to do what I want (for the most part)

Is it only my needs that are always met

What is the need

Is it greed when I give of myself cheerfully to others

Is it greed when I expect God in every aspect of my life

What is the need

Are you getting what you need
Or
Are you fulfilling your greed

Do not conform to the pattern of this world but be transformed by the renewing of your mind. Then you will be able to test and approve what God's will is his good, pleasing and perfect will. – Romans 12:2

NOTES

NOTES

NOTES

NOTES

NOTES

If we
CONFESS OUR SINS,
he is
faithful and just
and will FORGIVE US
our sins and
purify us
FROM ALL
UNRIGHTEOUSNESS.
– 1 John 1:9

Repentance

First has to start with the admission
Admission of what it is we did

Not denial to avoid the trial
Admission of what we knew in spite of what we do
Admission is the only way to get rid of what we did

Admission not to fellow man
Yet
Self to learn
Grow
And
Move on from

Without Admission to self
Repeat
Repeat
Repeatedly is the hindrance
That you will not be able to rebel

The enemy will use this to no avail
No matter how much you try to rebel

Repentance is the key
Yet
Admission turns the lock
And
Opens the door to release
Skeletons no more

Repent, Admit, Forgive and Release
And
Repeat.........

Life is so much more enjoyable
when we allow ourselves to travel light.

Whoever conceals their sins does not prosper, but the one who confesses and renounces them finds mercy.
– Proverbs 28:13

NOTES

NOTES

NOTES

NOTES

NOTES

OUR DAILY Bread

Get up

Get up

There is work to do

Heed my words when I am talking to you

You will know my voice when speaking to you

I am like no other who will ever be known

My father is the one who is on the throne

He reigns over you and me

Don't allow the devil the victory

Fight him with all your might

Pray, Fast, Deliver me!

I will hear your call and I will never let you fall

Don't allow yourself to be deceived by what you think you believe

My words are not few and my solutions are many

Rely on them, apply them, live within the Word

Have faith, not in what you believe, to be true
Yet
in the Everlasting Bread
I will continually give to you

And Jesus said to them, "I am the bread of life. He who comes to Me shall never hunger, and he who believes in Me shall never thirst. – John 6:35

NOTES

NOTES

NOTES

NOTES

NOTES

A life ending
Or
A life beginning

A life lived
Or
A life that has been forgiven

Death

A life saved
Or
A life praised

Death

Does death have a beginning
That never ends

Each person that dies is lived
On
Through many, even within sin

Through features
Characteristic
Ways good and bad
Sometimes not even knowing why they are had

Death stands for a:
Deliberate
Eternal
Appearance
That (1)
Has

Death only appears eternal because we can not imagine, see, believe or accept what comes after, what we can not experience.

Death is not a life once had
Yet
A life that keeps on giving
Even though it may make us feel sad

I am the living bread that came down from heaven. Whoever eats this bread will live forever. This bread is my flesh, which I will give for the life of the world.
– John 6:51

NOTES

NOTES

NOTES

NOTES

NOTES

Children are a
Heritage
from the Lord,
offspring a
Reward
from him.
– Psalm 127:3

A baby is a precious gift from God
Risen
then
Sent

Sent to be a seed that will grow much like a weed
Yet
Unlike a weed, this seed would be given two
To nurture and protect for all the world to view

This seed will have an identity much like a We

Sometimes you will like what you see
and
Sometimes you will say " You're nothing like me"

Yet, oh how the view will change

One day a blossoming flower the next,
oh how I need an hour

An hour to pause, just to find a cause
What was I thinking or was I thinking at all

Then reality hits
What would I do without you

Nothing at all
because
You are now the us that we both can see
The us that makes up the We
The we that others may stride to be

The us that now without you
We could never imagine
This new
We have
Has been a blessing from thee.

No discipline seems pleasant at the time, but painful. Later on, however, it produces a harvest of righteousness and peace for those who have been trained by it. – Hebrews 12:11

NOTES

NOTES

NOTES

NOTES

NOTES

Blessed is the one who
perseveres
under trial because, having stood the test,
that person will receive the
crown of life
that the Lord has promised to
those who love him. – James 1:12

Going In

Sometimes you have to go in
To get your breakthrough

You go in, to get through

To know God will always see you through

Don't just go through
Yet
Get beyond a breakthrough

Yet
Healing to be a revealing
Of
Why you went through

The other side has knowledge
That will keep and sustain you

Greater is he that I rely on
Than he that came to defeat me

He who lies cheats and tries to steal My Victory

No more holding back
Ohhhhh,
Yes
I will be going in

Going in, to get mine

Shouting and Praising my victory in

I have already won, because

God said, "It is So"
So now, I know
"It is done"

Consider it pure joy, my brothers and sisters, whenever you face trials of many kinds, because you know that the testing of your faith produces perseverance. Let perseverance finish its work so that you may be mature and complete, not lacking anything.
– James 1:2-4

NOTES

NOTES

NOTES

NOTES

NOTES

Your purpose in life was placed upon you in the womb
to see far beyond what you would be able to consume.

The moon and the stars that sit in the heavens above
did not even know this **wondrous love.**

God designed you with a spirit of love
that is found only when you are able to **ascend to above.**

A child born out of pain would be able to reveal to others their pain
and be able **to prophecy** what the heavens have sealed.

What only the heavens know to be, is truly real.
The Holy Prophetic word is what you are able to speak.

The stars and moon would be the only ones to **know** what you reveal.

You were formed to speak to nations and worldwide
not out of pride yet of the tide that would be felt worldwide.

The Messiah, Messiah, **Messiah**
there is work left to do.

Come ye, let me teach you the work of many yet few will be willing to do.
The **battle** has yet to be won but I tell you, the war has begun.

This is my warning, take heed
this is far more than the ability to **just believe.**

Your faith has to sustain what your belief
does not have the substance to believe.

I am not a mere man **to be explained.**

I am the power that comes from the Holy name,
which I was called into existence **to proclaim.**

I was called by God's power
to walk and speak to you **through God's appeal.**

The great I am says I am who he says I am
and to you, **God is revealed.**

You should heed God's voice **through me**.

I am a wonder to all but God,
so try not to figure out what you are not meant to be
yet, I am says the Lord because he made me.

God designed me for his purpose alone.

Believe my words because they come from a place you want to belong to.

A resting place of **eternal peace**; that is my home.

I am called by no other name than what **God has proclaimed**
Prophet K.C. Sparks is my name.

There is much more in a name than letters placed in vain.
S is for Spirit placed by God.
P is for Prophet that I was called to be.
A is for an arena that the world is to me.
R is for the responsibility which rests upon me.
K is for the kindness that God gives to me.
S is for the stars in people that God reveals to me.

Oh, **I am much greater than a name**
I am in line with the stars to be able to speak what God has proclaimed.

To miss **the prophetic words** revealed to me
is to miss what **God has ordained** as your destiny.

Recognize and obey, the Messiah will always have the last say.

Therefore tell the people: This is what the Lord Almighty says: 'Return to me,' declares the Lord Almighty, 'and I will return to you,' says the Lord Almighty. Do not be like your ancestors, to whom the earlier prophets proclaimed: This is what the Lord Almighty says: 'Turn from your evil ways and your evil practices.' But they would not listen or pay attention to me, declares the Lord. Where are your ancestors now? And the prophets, do they live forever? But did not my words and my decrees, which I commanded my servants the prophets, overtake your ancestors? – Zachariah 1: 3-5

NOTES

NOTES

NOTES

NOTES

CLOSING Remarks

These poems can not only be verified by the word of God, they can also be witnessed. I invite you to participate in the blessing of the Lord by joining me in fellowship and worship at FaithWalk Ministries in Paris, Missouri.

With your purchase, you are sowing a seed into Kingdom work. Fifty percent of all proceeds go back to God, from which it came. Some may be wondering – why fifty percent instead of ten percent, as the word saith? Yes – ten percent is from me, and the other forty percent is from you! My prayer is as Proverbs 11:28: "He who trusts in his riches will fall, but the righteous will flourish like foliage." So prepare yourself for your harvest! The seed has been sown.

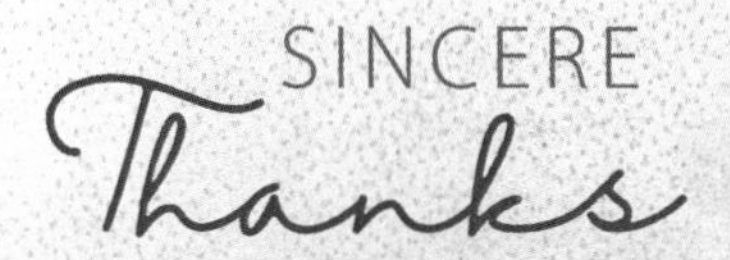

SINCERE Thanks

First, I would like to give thanks and honor to God, for this is one of the many gifts that the Lord has blessed me with. I would like to thank everyone who encouraged me and prayed for this manifestation of God. I am extending an extra special thank you to Holy Ground in Fayette MO, Steven Sr. , Steven Jr., Spencer and Shadora for accepting and loving me as their mother and granny, as different as I am. Yet also special to Him.

And when they had *prayed* the place where they were assembled together was *shaken* and they were all *filled with the Holy Spirit* and they spoke the *word of God* with *boldness*. – Acts 4:31

Made in the USA
San Bernardino, CA
23 February 2020

64802396R00049